February 1984

G*reetings and peace to all of you,*

Catholics of this Archdiocese, faithful and catechumens, for whom I pray daily as your Archbishop.

I have often written and spoken to you briefly about various aspects of our work as a Church and have asked for your support. Now I want to write at greater length, not just about our work but about our life. In speaking of the liturgy, I hope to reach and touch the spirit of prayer in your hearts—that spirit which brings us together each Sunday for the Eucharist. And I also have in mind those of you whom infirmity prevents from joining physically in the celebration: Your prayer is part of every Mass we celebrate.

In December 1963, the Second Vatican Council completed its first document, the *Constitution on the Sacred Liturgy.* Some of you remember that time very clearly, but others have grown up in the Church since then. In honor of the twentieth anniversary, I want to speak to both: those who, like myself, knew the forms of liturgy set 400 years ago and those who cannot remember the Mass in Latin, the "last gospel," the altar against the wall.

Most often when you and I meet, we celebrate the liturgy. As we do, I realize more and more fully the truth of that great insight of the bishops at Vatican II: "In the liturgy the whole public worship is performed by the Mystical Body of Jesus Christ, that is, by the Head and His members" (*Constitution on the Sacred Liturgy, #7*). The liturgy is the action of God's assembled people.

In the past we often spoke as if the bishop or the priest alone celebrated the liturgy. But the evidence and the bishops' words at Vatican II are strong and definite: Whenever we gather as the Church—for Sunday Mass, for anointing the sick, for burying the dead—we celebrate the liturgy together. The *General Instruction on the Roman Missal* puts it simply: "The celebration of Mass is the action of Christ and the people of God . . ." (#1).

We call this gathered Church "assembly." It is you and it is I. Bishops, priests, and deacons have unique roles in celebrating the liturgy, but they act as persons who serve the assembled people.

It is good theology and also good common sense, a matter learned not so much from documents and textbooks as from experience, that the assembled Church celebrates the liturgy. I learned this saying family prayers in my home and at evening devotions in my parish church. I learned it also in these last two decades which have been a time of renewal, making it more clear that the liturgy, while Christ's action first, of course, is also the action of God's people, who sing, listen to the scripture, praise and thank God, greet one another in peace, and share in the holy

communion of Christ and the Church.

This letter about the liturgy is sent to all of you, for you are the people who celebrate our liturgy; you are the assembly. In writing it I take for granted observance of all the Church's liturgical norms, which provide a positive framework encouraging us to engage in creative, authentic celebration of the liturgy.

Twenty years is very little time for so profound an experience to take hold, but at this point it is useful for us to ask ourselves how we are doing. I am going to ask you that, and ask it in a number of ways. I am going to chide a bit and challenge a lot. But I must say three things by way of introduction.

Introduction

First, thank you. I say that to all those who have labored to make the liturgy strong and beautiful: ushers, artists, musicians, writers, planners, lectors, cantors, deacons, servers, communion ministers, priests, sacristans – all who have accepted any ministry of service to the people of the parishes. Thanks especially to you who simply come to take your places and celebrate the Mass week after week.

The Church in Chicago is known throughout the United States and even beyond for liturgical leadership which began long before Vatican II. In 1940 the first of those national gatherings that became known as "Liturgical Weeks" was held at our cathedral. Priests, religious and laity who studied and worked through these years helped prepare the way for the renewal that came from the Council. Over the years, outstanding members of the Chicago Church have shown by teaching and example what parish liturgy can be. I am thankful for all this work and zeal.

A second thing I must say simply to be certain we have a common foundation, a shared understanding of the liturgy. I understand the liturgy to be those rituals in which the Church assembled expresses its very life. In our rituals we give thanks to God – for thanksgiving is the day-in, day-out attitude of the baptized; we intercede – for we are baptized to hold up all creation's needs to God; we read our sacred book, the Bible, and sing from our prayerbook, the psalms—for those words and prayers accompany us from childhood to old age.

From our parents and grandparents we have received the rites by which we give thanks, intercede, anoint and confirm, marry and bury. We do them over and over, and we teach our children to do them. Thus do we discover what it is to be a Christian and a Catholic. We learn this in hearing the word of God, in the hymns and acclamations, in the genuflections and the kneeling, in the greeting of peace, in sharing the consecrated bread and wine at the holy table. The liturgy is not an "extra," something nice that may give us good feelings. It is our life, our very spirit. It is the source of our identity and renewal as a Church.

When we let the liturgy shape us—from the ashes of Lent and the waters of baptism to the broken bread and poured out cup at every Sunday's Mass—then we shall find what it is "to put on Christ."

Yet liturgy is also a humble reality, and participation in liturgy

does not exhaust our duties as Christians. We shall be judged for attending to justice and giving witness to the truth, for hungry people fed and prisoners visited. Liturgy itself does not do these things. Yet good liturgy makes us a people whose hearts are set on such deeds. Liturgy is our communion, our strength, our nourishment, our song, our peace, our reminder, our promise. This singular meeting with the Lord Jesus leads us to make all the events and circumstances of our lives occasions for meeting Him. Liturgy is for me the bedrock of all my prayer and the measure of all my deeds.

My last introductory note is this: Over and over the Council stressed that the great goal for liturgical renewal is our "full, conscious and active participation in liturgical celebrations which is demanded by the very nature of the liturgy" (*Constitution on the Sacred Liturgy,* #14). Since those words were written we have only begun. The liturgical books have been revised so that the liturgy may indeed be celebrated in this way. But revising books and changing language does not make it happen. There is need for

excellence on the part of all who minister at the liturgy, with all the artistry and hard work that entails. And yet even that is pointless until all who assemble to celebrate the liturgy have it in mind to participate together in this sacred deed.

The commitment I envision must be in our Catholic bones: the need to assemble each Sunday, to make common prayer in song, to hear the scriptures and reflect on them, to intercede for all the world, to gather at the holy table and give God thanks and praise over the bread and wine which are for us the body and blood of our Lord Jesus Christ, and finally to go from that room to our separate worlds – but now carrying the tune we have heard, murmuring the words we have made ours, nourished by the sacred banquet, ready in so many ways to make all God's creation and all the work of human hands into the kingdom we have glimpsed in the liturgy.

In 1978 the U.S. bishops reminded us that "God does not need liturgy, people do" (*Environment and Art in Catholic Worship,* #4). It is not an option, nor merely an obligation, not a bonus but a need – like food and drink, like sleep and work, like friends. "God does not need liturgy, people do." We need to gather, listen, give praise and thanks, share communion. Otherwise, we forget who we are and whose we are; we have neither the strength nor joy to be Christ's body present in today's world.

It is true of course – and indeed, this is a central truth about the Mass and sacraments – that the action performed is first and foremost Christ's. It is He who renews His act of perfect fidelity to the Father's will, He who welcomes new members into the community of the Church, He who forgives and reconciles. In that sense, even liturgy "badly" celebrated is efficacious. Nevertheless, the quality of *our* participation, of *our* action, is also important; that quality, in fact, enhances our participation in the action of Christ. Liturgy is not magic; we must bring to it the very best of which we are capable.

Although the liturgy expresses our whole life – our birth in baptism, our growth and forgiveness in reconciliation – here I shall speak only of the Sunday Eucharist because it is our usual and regular way of gathering. How do you and I celebrate the liturgy each Sunday? If the liturgy is something done by the assembled people of the parish, how are we doing this task of ours?

I ask you to read what follows in a very practical spirit, thinking of your own parish and the Sunday Eucharist there, and especially of your own participation in that Mass.

On Sunday, How Do We Gather?

Everything that happens before the first scripture reading is meant to help us assemble. That means gathering together many individuals as one community at prayer, but it also means recollecting ourselves personally — not by leaving behind the cares and distractions of home and work, but by bringing them into the gospel's light.

So we gather, one by one, household by household, passing through the doors of this parish church of ours, greeting one another, taking our places. This building called a "church" is a kind of living room of the family of God — it is *our* room when we assemble as the Church. Here we are at home.

Its style differs from parish to parish. Its architecture and decoration may be in one tradition or another. What matters most is that the room allows us all to gather closely, see one another's faces, be truly present to one another. The common focus is the holy table and near it the chair of the presider and the stand where the scriptures are read. But liturgy is not a performance, and we are no audience. Liturgy is an activity, and the room itself should help this happen. Many directives make it clear that in building new churches and renovating old ones it is important to bear in mind our need to see and hear one another, even as we see and hear the priest, the reader, the cantor.

But even the best architecture can only invite us to come together and pray together. That invitation must be accepted. Certainly there are times for praying alone, seeking privacy, but the Sunday liturgy is not one of these. The first task of each one who comes on Sunday for liturgy is to take the open place nearest to the holy table. Let our churches fill from the front to the back, and if there are empty places, let them be the ones farthest from the altar. The open places near the doors are then available for those who may hesitate to draw closer because of some private need or sense of alienation. Let them feel welcome whenever they come to the church.

Every parish has members who care for the beauty of the church building and the physical well-being of the assembly. Sacristans keep this house for the Church clean and beautiful. Working with artists, they prepare the room for special feasts and for the seasons. Ushers help people find places, and are truly servants of the assembly. They are models of the hospitality we should all have as we greet one another.

One last note about these important moments before Mass. As members of the assembly, we should be there—we should be *assembled*—before the liturgy begins. Coming late or at the last minute, if that can be avoided, says we are only spectators dropping in to see a performance. But the liturgy is ours. To come late or leave early breaks the very spirit of the assembly. Come early instead, to greet others, to pray quietly, to center your thoughts on the Lord to whose table you have been invited. Come early and bring the concerns and problems that occupy you, all the people you carry in your heart.

How we begin the liturgy will vary somewhat from season to season and place to place. Always we make the sign of the cross, respond to the greeting of the one who presides, priest or bishop, and join in the opening prayer of the Mass. Usually we sing either an opening hymn or the "Lord, have mercy" or the Gloria. The familiar and lovely routine leads us into community prayer.

The sign of the cross should be made with reverence and attention. By this simple gesture we identify ourselves as Christians. This sign marked us even before baptism and will mark us even after death.

We respond to the presider's greeting and give him our full attention. When he extends the invitation, "Let us pray," we welcome the silent time to gather ourselves in stillness, so that we can enter fully into the opening prayer, unique to each Sunday, which places us in communion with the Church throughout the world.

Singing within the entrance rite is a wonderful way for us to realize that we are a *community* at prayer. Cantors and those who play musical instruments select and gradually teach people those compositions which will draw forth their song. Here, and throughout the liturgy, music is not a decoration but part of the central action itself. What we do in liturgy is too vast and too deep to be left to our speaking voices. We need music so that we can fully express what we are about.

As the one who presides over the assembly, the priest has an important service to render in these introductory moments. Standing by his chair, he gives us his full attention as he leads us in the sign of the cross, greets us, and invites us to join in the opening prayer. Additional words, if any, should be very few, so that the cross, the greeting, and the prayer stand out and are not rushed.

How the entrance rite gathers us and prepares us for word and Eucharist will vary from one liturgical season to another. Art, music, and words themselves tell us that we are again in Advent or Christmastime, in Lent or Eastertime, or in the Sundays of Ordinary Time. Commentaries and explanations should be superfluous.

If we gather as we ought – singing together, being silent together, responding together – we will be a community praying, and know that we are such.

How Do We Listen to the Word?

From the first reading through the prayers of intercession we are engaged in the liturgy of the word. Most of our "doing" at this part of the Mass is listening. On Sundays we listen to three readings from the scriptures and the homily.

This kind of listening is not passive – it is something *we do*. At these moments in the Mass the liturgical action is not just reading

and preaching, *it is listening.* Readers and homilist are servants to
the listening assembly.

Often, though, we do not listen very well. Listening is a skill
that grows dull in the barrage of words one hears all day long. Yet
we have no substitute for it. In the liturgy we are schooled in the art
of listening. What we do here, we are to do with our lives – be good
listeners to one another, to the Lord, to the world with all its needs.

We usually have a reading from the Hebrew Scriptures, one
from the writings of the New Testament, and one from the gospels. Every three years the Church reads through most of the four
gospels, much of the New Testament, and scattered selections
from the Old Testament. The scripture selections themselves
shape the liturgical seasons of Advent, Christmastime, Lent, and
Eastertime. During the rest of the year we generally read straight
through the gospels and letters, picking up each week where we
left off the week before.

The Council used the image of a pilgrimage in speaking of the
Church. We are on a journey, not only as individuals but as a
Church living out corporate life down through the centuries. On
this journey we carry a book, our scriptures. Each week we gather,
and in our midst the book is opened and read. Its words are heard
over and over again. They have come down to us through dozens
and even hundreds of generations. We in turn read them to another
generation and so entrust the book to our children. In these stories,
visions, poems, letters – all sorts of writing – we Christians find
again and again the meaning of our own journey, the Lord who is
our way and truth and life.

Our listening, then, is not like listening to a lecture, not like
listening to a play. It is listening with the whole self, mind and
heart and soul. We do not expect to be entertained or to learn new
facts, but to hear God's word proclaimed simply and with power:
the word of God spoken again to the *Church.*

What helps us listen? Several things are important.

First: Lectors, deacons, and priests must read as the story-
tellers of the community. Entrusted with a sacred possession, our

scriptures, they must live and pray with their scripture reading during the week before, practicing over and over, making it their own. They need to be capable of holding the attention of the assembly through their mastery of technical skills and also through their deep love for God's word and His people.

It is a delight and an inspiration to me when I hear good lectors, women and men faithful to their task and trying to improve their skills. They truly struggle with God's word. Story and storyteller become one. Deacons and priests, as readers of the gospel, must work just as hard. The lives of all who read publicly should embody the words they proclaim.

The second element for good listening is this: Unless you have difficulty in hearing, I suggest that you give full attention to the reader and not rely on a booklet or hymnal containing the scripture texts. A reader lacks inducement to read as well as possible if others are following their own texts, for then the bond of communication is broken. We should fix our eyes on the reader and give full attention to the living word.

Third: It would be well if all of us who listen to the scriptures on Sunday prepared by reading scripture at home during the week – especially by studying and reflecting on the texts we will hear on the following Sunday.

Fourth and last: At the liturgy, the readings are to be surrounded with reverence, with honor. This means many things: reverent use of a beautiful lectionary, a period of silence after the first and second readings and after the homily, singing the psalm between the first two readings, a sung acclamation of the gospel. These are to be part of the normal pattern for Sunday Mass in our parishes.

The psalm is especially important. As we chant its refrain, we are learning the Church's most basic prayerbook. The cantor is the minister who leads this sung prayer. While singing the psalm is perhaps not yet possible at all parish Masses, we can strive with all urgency to train parish cantors. The reintroduction of this ministry is one of the finest developments of the last two decades. The lectionary permits use of the same psalm over a number of weeks so that people can become familiar with it. Gradually learning the psalm refrains by heart in the Sunday assembly, we can make them part of our morning or evening prayer each day.

We all recognize how important the homily is. You want good homilies; you need good homilies; you deserve good homilies. As parishioners, then, you must give your priests the time to prepare. Priests and deacons must both ask for that time (allowing others to take on various ministries in the parish) and then use the time well.

The homily is the assembly's conversation with the day's scripture readings. Only by respecting both scripture and the community can the homilist speak for and to the assembly, bringing it together in this time and place with this Sunday's scriptures. Good homilists must be familiar with the community's needs, pains and hopes. They must challenge and encourage. And they must seek out and listen to parishioners' comments. Those who preach should make frequent use of seminars and classes on homiletics and scripture.

Except for the most serious reason, the homily should not depart from the season and the scriptures. Homilies flow from the scriptures just heard, not from some other series of topics or themes. This is not a limitation on the content of homilies, for homilists who pay close attention to the cycle of readings will find ample opportunity to preach on the whole breadth of the gospel as it relates to contemporary life.

The reforms which followed Vatican II reintroduced the prayer of the faithful (the general intercessions) into the Roman liturgy. This prayer is a litany: One after another the needs of the world and the Church are brought before the assembly, and to each we respond with prayer. When the intercessions are sung and the assembly responds to each with the singing of "Lord, hear our prayer" or "Lord, have mercy," it is clear that the intercessions are made by the people. Many of us remember how beautiful and strong a litany prayer can be when sung. The repetition of the chanted response reinforces the urgency of our appeal, and we realize our common priesthood in Jesus Christ, placing constantly before God all the troubles and needs of this earth.

How Do We Give Praise and Thanks?

Between the liturgy of the word and the liturgy of the Eucharist we have some rather quiet, practical moments. The collection is taken and the gifts and table are prepared.

The collection itself is, according to the *General Instruction on the Roman Missal*, "for the poor and the church" (#49). Bread and wine are brought by the faithful, but so are gifts of money. This is a true part of the liturgy. In this way we place what we have earned by our work within the holy time of Mass. Unwilling ever to separate our lives from our prayer, we bring something for the poor and the Church from our wealth or our poverty.

Now for the first time in the liturgy, our attention is focused on the altar. We bring bread and wine to be placed there along with the book of prayers. The unleavened bread is obviously not our usual bread but a simple bread, a bread of the poor. In this bread we cast our lot with the poor, knowing ourselves – however materially affluent – to be poor people, needy, hungry. Unless we acknowledge our hunger, we have no place at this table. How else can God feed us? Ideally, because the bread is so important, enough should be brought forward and consecrated each time for all the people at that Mass.

We also bring forward wine. Like bread, it is "fruit of the earth and work of human hands," something simple, something from our tables, a drink of ordinary delight.

When the table has been prepared, we stand and are invited to lift up our hearts to the Lord and give Him thanks and praise. Thus begins the eucharistic prayer in which we do indeed give thanks to God our Creator for all the work of salvation, but especially for the paschal mystery, that passover of Jesus whereby dying He destroyed our death and rising He restored our life. The priest proclaims this prayer, but "the whole congregation joins Christ in acknowledging the works of God and in offering the sacrifice" (*General Instruction*, #54).

So this eucharistic prayer, too, is the work of the assembly. That must be clear in the way we pray it. There is an immense challenge here. Centuries of practice shaped the assembly as spectators rather than participants. We who are older grew up understanding ourselves as lone individuals deriving what we could from prayer and adoration while the sacred action took place at the altar. But we are a holy people, called to praise God actively for His saving action in our lives.

In every eucharistic prayer the whole assembly joins the proclamation of praise led by the priest. By singing the "Holy, holy," the memorial acclamation, and the "Amen," we claim the prayer as our own. These acclamations are so important that even if we sing nothing else at the Mass, we sing these affirmations of faith. Every parish should have a number of melodies for them which everyone can sing by heart.

Nine texts for the eucharistic prayer have been approved in English. Priests and liturgy planners should be thoroughly familiar with them, so as to choose the prayer best suited to each season or Sunday.

These eucharistic prayers express in words the action we perform. All of us are becoming familiar with them. In the words of the old Roman Canon (now the first eucharistic prayer), Christ is present "for us," to bring us "every grace and blessing." In our newer prayers, "every grace and blessing" is spelled out in clearer detail. We thank God "for counting us worthy to stand in your presence and serve you," and ask that "all of us who share in the body and blood of Christ be brought together in unity by the Holy Spirit" (Eucharistic Prayer II); Christ is present upon the altar so that we may be filled with the Holy Spirit, "and become one body, one spirit in Christ" (Eucharistic Prayer III); we pray that we ourselves will become "a living sacrifice of praise" (Eucharistic Prayer IV). Renewed by the Holy Spirit, we lift up all the elements of life in praise and offer ourselves to be spent in sacrifice.

We are called to the Lord's table less for solace than for strength, not so much for comfort as for service. This prayer, then,

is prayed not only over the bread and wine, so that they become Christ's body and blood for us to share; it is prayed over the entire assembly so that we may become the dying and risen Christ for the world. Participation in this great prayer of praise, as meal and sacrifice, transforms us. By grace, we more and more become what we pray.

The voice and manner of the priest should show that he offers this prayer as spokesman for everyone present. It is a *prayer* addressed to the Father. Not a homily or a drama or a talk given to the assembly, it embraces remembrance of God's saving deeds, invocation of the Holy Spirit, the narrative of the Last Supper, remembrance of the Church universal and of the dead, and climaxes "through Him, with Him, in Him . . ."

For all our devotion to the body and blood of Christ present on our altars, we Catholics have hardly begun to make this eucharistic prayer the heart of the liturgy. It is still, to all appearances, a monologue by the priest, who stops several times to let the people sing. We seem as yet to have little sense for the flow, the

movement, the beauty of the eucharistic prayer. How are we to make our own this prayer which is the summit and center of the Church's whole life? How are we to see that this prayer is the model of Christian life and daily prayer? Does this prayer of thanks and praise gather up the way we pray by ourselves every day? When we assemble on Sunday, we help one another learn over and over again how to praise and thank God through and with and in Christ, in good and bad times, until He comes in glory.

Are we a thanks-giving people? Do we give God praise by morning and thanks by night? Do we pause over every table before eating, as we do over this altar table, to bless God and ourselves and our food? The habit of thanksgiving, of praise, of Eucharist, must be acquired day by day, not just at Sunday Mass. In fact, it is at Mass that our habits of daily life come to full expression in Christ.

What Is Our Communion?

The communion rite begins with the Lord's Prayer and the peace greeting, continues through the "Lamb of God" as the consecrated bread is broken, moves into the communion procession, and concludes with silent and spoken prayer. Here it is clear that the assembly performs the liturgy; all of us pray the Lord's Prayer, exchange the sign of peace, and join in the litany "Lamb of God," and all are invited to partake of communion.

In their recent letter on *The Challenge of Peace: God's Promise and Our Response*, the bishops of the United States wrote that "we encourage every Catholic to make the sign of peace at Mass an authentic sign of our reconciliation with God and with one another. This sign of peace is also a visible sign of our commitment to work for peace as a Christian community. We approach the table of the Lord only after having dedicated ourselves as a Christian community to peace and reconciliation." So let it be in our parishes. When we greet those around us, let our words and manner speak of Christ's peace.

In the first decades of the Church the Sunday gathering was

known simply as the "breaking of the bread." That gesture seemed to say everything. The loaf was divided and shared so that many might eat and become one. After our peace greeting has signified how we stand with those around us and with all the Church, we attend to the priest as he lifts up the large host and breaks it.

Following the invitation to the table and the response ("Lord, I am not worthy . . ."), the communion procession begins. The communion of priest, deacon and communion ministers should never take so long that the communion of the people cannot follow directly on the invitation.

In most of our parishes now auxiliary ministers of communion assist the priest and deacon in taking communion to the people. This helps make it clear that we are *together* at this table, that this communion is the very image of the Church and of that kingdom for which we live and die. Ushers contribute to the dignity and reverence of this sacred moment by helping the assembled community form a true procession and by offering assistance to those who may need it, such as the elderly, the infirm and the very young.

At this table we put aside every worldly separation based on culture, class, or other differences. Baptized, we no longer admit to distinctions based on age or sex or race or wealth. This communion is why all prejudice, all racism, all sexism, all deference to wealth and power must be banished from our parishes, our homes, and our lives. This communion is why we will not call enemies those who are human beings like ourselves. This communion is why we will not commit the world's resources to an escalating arms race while the poor die. We cannot. Not when we have feasted here on the "body broken" and "blood poured out" for the life of the world.

Let that be clear in the reverent way we walk forward to take the holy bread and cup. Let it be clear in the way ministers of communion announce: "The body of Christ," "The blood of Christ." Let it be clear in our "Amen!" Let it be clear in the songs and psalms we sing and the way we sing them. Let it be clear in the holy silence that fills this church when all have partaken.

Before coming forward we say, "Lord, I am not worthy." We are never worthy of this table, for it is God's grace and gift. Yet we do come forward. This is "food for the journey" that we began at baptism. We may eat of it when we are tired, when we are discouraged, even when we have failed. But not when we have forgotten the Church, forgotten the way we began at the font; not when we have abandoned our struggle against evil and remain unrepentant for having done so. Let us examine our lives honestly each time before approaching the Eucharist. "Worthy" none of us ever is, but properly prepared each one of us must be. Christ, present in the Eucharist and in us, calls us to be a holy communion, to grow in love and holiness for one another's sake.

When the priest is seated and the vessels have been quietly put aside, then stillness and peace are ours. Only after the meaning of the life we share has entered deeply into our souls does the presider rise to speak a final prayer.

What Does Our Dismissal Mean?

The concluding part of our Roman liturgy is very brief: the blessing and the sending forth. A procession through the assembly and a concluding song are usually part of this, but these are things the local parish needs to design for its own needs. Whatever is done in these final moments, including any announcements that have to be made, should help us pass from the moments of community ritual to less formal time together and then back to our own lives and daily prayers.

We are sent from the eucharistic table as a holy people always in mission. (The word "Mass" – in Latin *Missa* – means "sending" or "mission.") The spirit which fills us in the liturgy inspires us to re-create the world and in doing so to prepare ourselves for fulfillment in heaven.

In all we have done at Mass we have been uttering promises to one another, creating visions for one another, giving one another hope. Our hymns proclaim that faith is worth singing about. Our repentant prayers not only confess our own unworthiness but praise God's mercy and affirm our pledge to be merciful and seek reconciliation with all people. Our voices united in the acclamations express our willingness to be counted as witnesses to the gospel, with a mission to the world.

There is nothing narrow, selfish or blind in our Sunday worship. We give thanks not so much for personal favors from the Lord as for the earth itself, for the goodness of creation and the wonder of our senses, for the prophets and the saints and for our sisters and brothers throughout the earth, for God's saving deeds recorded in our scriptures and visible in our world. Only in such thanksgiving can we look on this world, embrace its sorrows and troubles, and confront the mystery of evil and suffering.

To give praise to God in such a world is to proclaim our own baptism into the death and the resurrection of Christ, a baptism that marks us for continuing conversion, the work of Christ's Spirit in us. We have seen and will continue to see sorrow and evil, yet we go on struggling, with songs of praise to God on our lips. This is, as

Paul knew, nonsense to the world, but it is the way we have chosen. We are a people who lift up songs of thanks over bread and wine which become for us the true presence of Christ. His coming was proclaimed in Mary's Magnificat, a coming marked by the removal of the mighty from their thrones and the lifting up of the lowly, by the hunger of the rich and the satisfaction of the hungry. Only those who live out that proclamation daily discover finally why it is not a dirge that we sing when we gather but praise.

The dismissal of the assembly is like the breaking of the bread. We have become "the bread of life" and "the cup of blessing" for the world. Now we are scattered, broken, poured out to be life for the world. What happens at home, at work, at meals? What do we make of our time, our words, our deeds, our resources of all kinds? That is what matters.

Our Progress in Liturgy

I cannot reflect on the Eucharist without being aware of other concerns: how our celebration of Sunday Mass embodies our love for young children, our solidarity with the handicapped, our response to catechumens. I think, too, of that justice which we celebrate and to which we commit ourselves at Mass. How can we – in liturgy and in life – show the world a community where old age is loved and respected, where the sufferings of the poor are known and remedies are sought, where we can say with Paul that among us "there does not exist male or female but all are one in Christ Jesus"? I am conscious, too, of many matters of liturgical practice, among them: the unnecessarily large number of Sunday Masses celebrated in some parishes and how this adversely affects the quality of the liturgy; my encouragement for communion under both kinds as prescribed by liturgical norms; my strong support for the cultural diversity in the liturgies of Chicago's parishes – in language, music, and other expressions where it truly manifests the Christian spirit of the people.

All of these things are important to me. I will look for opportunities to speak of them in the future.

Whether you remember back before Vatican II or not, you know that these have not been easy years. We have had our problems in the liturgy. Where the Spirit of God breathes, there can be human excess, either of enthusiasm or reluctance. Liturgical renewal, like any other renewal, would be inauthentic without the mystery of the cross. Some have seen our liturgy as a mere means to teach or propagandize, some have trivialized it with unworthy songs and themes and needless comments and explanations, and some – perhaps saddest of all – have taken the renewed liturgy only as a set of directions, a kind of operating manual. One result of this last attitude has been to make the liturgy something mechanical and lifeless; the songs and words and gestures and the whole flow of the Mass fail to convey that this is indeed the action of the assembly.

Perhaps all that had to be. But now we need to ask: Are we ready for a deeper and more lasting approach to our Sunday Mass? Are we priests ready to work at presiding, to work at being members and leaders of the assembly?

Are we all, priests and parishioners, ready to say that the parish's commitment to liturgy may mean spending time and money? How else can we train good liturgical ministers? How else can we support staff people as coordinators of liturgy? How else can we pay just salaries to trained musicians who work with all aspects of liturgical music—with choirs, instrumentalists and organists, cantors and groups specializing in one or another style of music? How else can we build or renovate places of worship to make them truly "the house of the Church," fitting places for us to assemble, listen, give thanks, and share communion?

During these twenty years, much of the liturgical renewal seems to have been concerned with external changes. The approach was practical. The revised books that have followed from the *Constitution on the Sacred Liturgy* have given us a marvelous form for our prayer. Now we need to make this liturgy ours, to be at home with it, to know it deeply, to let it shape our everyday lives. Further changes in rubrics and wording may indeed come, but our present task is to make beautiful and make our own the tradition we have received.

I encourage all of you, especially the clergy and all others involved in various ministries at the liturgy, to mark the twentieth anniversary of the *Constitution on the Sacred Liturgy* in one very special way: Read it, read it again. When I go back to that initial work of Vatican II, I see what came from the liturgical movement, the courage of Pope John XXIII and the determination of the world's bishops—and the Holy Spirit working in all of them.

Conclusion

You know by now that I love the liturgy and find my own identity there, as well as yours and that of the whole Church. How glad I would be to see all of us delighted and inspired by every Sunday Mass in every parish! But good liturgy cannot be created out of a bishop's letters or rules. I can only call you to be what Christ has already called you to be. I can only invite you to serve God and one another in the beauty and depth of Sunday Mass. I can only hold up some goals and ideals, and pledge my own best efforts and the support of the archdiocese. I can only keep you and the liturgy of your parishes in my own prayer.

Above all else, you must know, as I do, that we learn to pray by praying. Can we take the treasure of prayer that is ours and begin – alone or together – to pray as the Church each morning and night? Can we keep Sunday holy? Can we take the Sunday scriptures and other passages of scripture into each week and even each day? Can we heed the bishops' call in our letter on peace – the call for prayer and fasting and abstinence on Fridays? Can we keep the great seasons of Advent and Christmas, Lent and Eastertime, not only in our churches but in our homes? Only in these ways will we gradually become active members of a Sunday assembly of the baptized who know how to gather, how to listen to the word, how to give thanks and praise, how to share in holy communion, how to take leave of one another for the week-long and life-long work of building the kingdom of kindness, justice, and peace.

Joseph Cardinal Bernardin

ARCHBISHOP OF CHICAGO